Boxing Mastery

Advanced Technique, Tactics and Strategies from the Sweet Science

Mark Hatmaker
with Doug Werner

Tracks Publishing
San Diego, California

Photography by
Doug Werner

TRACKS
PUBLISHING

Boxing Mastery
Advanced Technique, Tactics and Strategies from the Sweet Science

Mark Hatmaker with Doug Werner

Tracks Publishing
458 Dorothy Avenue
Ventura, CA 93003
805-754-0248
tracks@cox.net
www.startupsports.com

All rights reserved. No part of this book may be reproduced or transmitted in any form or by any means, electronic or mechanical, including photocopying, recording or by any information storage and retrieval system without permission from the author, except for the inclusion of brief quotations in a review.

Copyright © 2004 by Doug Werner

10 9 8 7 6 5

Hatmaker, Mark.
    Boxing mastery : advanced technique, tactics and strategies from the sweet science / Mark Hatmaker with Doug Werner.
    p. cm.
    Includes index.
    ISBN 1884654215
    LCCN 2004111980

    1. Boxing--Training.   I. Werner, Doug, 1950-
II. Title.

GV1137.6.H38 2004   796.83
                      QBI04-700438

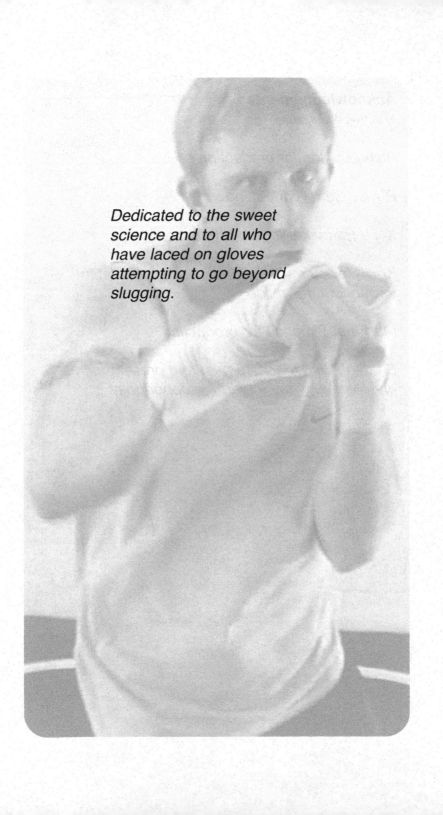

Dedicated to the sweet science and to all who have laced on gloves attempting to go beyond slugging.

Acknowledgements
in alphabetical order

Aisha Buxton for production

Phyllis Carter for editing

Kylie Hatmaker for set production

Kory Hays for showing and sharing his talent throughout this guide

Margaret Simonds for production

Students and teachers past and present for making every day a learning opportunity

Contents

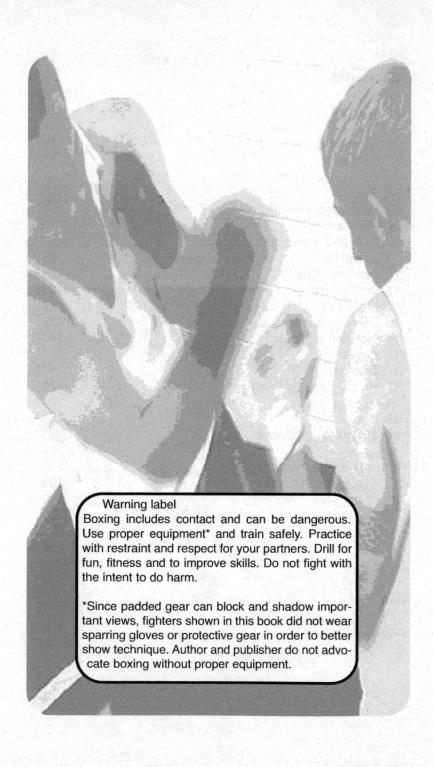

Warning label

Boxing includes contact and can be dangerous. Use proper equipment* and train safely. Practice with restraint and respect for your partners. Drill for fun, fitness and to improve skills. Do not fight with the intent to do harm.

*Since padded gear can block and shadow important views, fighters shown in this book did not wear sparring gloves or protective gear in order to better show technique. Author and publisher do not advocate boxing without proper equipment.

Introduction

If you browse any bookstore looking for contemporary boxing books, you will find a few biographies of past great fighters and a smattering from the present. You will find also many titles regarding fitness boxing. Fitness boxing is a curious animal. It is nothing more than taking the bare bones of the professional boxer's conditioning regimen and cleaning it up for mass consumption. Fitness boxing removes the bumps and bruises and glosses over the hard-core approach to a fighter's training program. The result is a toothless bastardization of a noble sport.

I understand the urge and visceral attraction to becoming fit by going though the motions that truly tough human beings perform. But most of these workout books are pale imitations of the real thing and poorly represent the sweet science. These contemporary volumes may show you some punches and a few combinations, but they have removed the science from the sweet science.

With the exception of the two fine volumes by Doug Werner and Alan Lachica, *Boxer's Start-Up* and *Fighting Fit* (Tracks Publishing) you will find little to nothing in print that covers the deceptive tactics, strategies and advanced maneuverings of the fight game. *Boxing Mastery* reintroduces the scientific and strategic beauty of the sport above fitness and slugging. I seek to put the brain back into the athlete who wants to use his entire body to best effect.

This book is intended for the fighter who already knows the basics. If you are a novice, there is much to be learned here, but I urge you to take a look at the two boxing titles listed in the Resources section as well as the recommended video instruction. *Boxing Mastery* is intended to be a source book of strategies and tactics for the real boxer — the individual who wants to take the sport beyond a trendy cardio activity and test his mettle with an actual opponent.

You will not find every tactic and tip ever accrued in the ring between these covers. That would call for a much larger volume. You will find plenty to mull over, whether you're green to the ring or have pro fights to your credit. Training equipment, conditioning, speed bag work, double-end bag tips, maize ball drills, rope-skipping, plyometric exercises and the like are not included here. My primary task is to enlighten the fighter in the realm of ring generalship. And generalship it is. For boxing is more than survival of the fittest. It is a game of conditioned reflex action, destructive deception and coordinated, exquisitely articulated physical combat. Indeed, boxing is a science. And a sweet one at that.

Lead and rear hands — a special note
Probably a first in the annals of boxing books, both fighters in this book (Mark Hatmaker and Kory Hays) are south-paws. No problem. Right and left leads will get the same benefit from this guide because hands are labeled lead and rear, not right or left. Read the material and as you look at the photos, adjust according to your preference.

1 The training continuum

There is a ton of information in these pages. If you are an experienced fighter, feel free to jump in anywhere. I recommend the novice start at the beginning and work through the end of the book. No matter your skill level, I recommend you take each technique or tactic and work it through the following training continuum to ensure that the information is deeply seated into your nervous system.

Mirror training
I know it is tempting to take a new idea and run immediately to the heavy bag or get in front of an opponent, but the most important piece of equipment you can own is a full-length mirror. The mirror is absolutely the best tool for self-correction. By working before a mirror, you provide your own feedback about your movement, technique and guard. Is as tight, fluid and powerful as need be? Work everything in front of the mirror — footwork, offense, defense and upper body movement. Keep this fact in mind: If it ain't right in front of the mirror, it ain't gonna be right anywhere else.

Equipment training

After you've honed your tools in front of the mirror, it is time to apply them to solid targets. Take the selected technique or tactic and apply it to the training apparatus that will best accomplish the desired result. In other words, select the device that will provide the most realistic feedback for that particular tool. In broad strokes, (there are exceptions) use the heavy bag for working power, the double-end bag for timing and accuracy, the maize bag for defense, slip-sticks for upper-body mobility and so on. With this information in mind, choose wisely.

Partner/coach drills

This vital step in the continuum allows you to stand before a live opponent who is either gloved up himself or outfitted with focus mitts. At this point in the game you are not sparring yet, but working the designated tool or tactic in isolation, preferably in real time.

Counterpunching drills

This is a complex aspect of the continuum that requires much forethought. It is an absolutely vital step in moving the fighter from being only a puncher into a boxer.

Situation and isolation sparring

Here you finally work with an opponent, but you are not slinging leather with abandon. You and your partner agree on ground rules that limit the usual boxing game in order to emphasize the tool or tactic to be drilled. For example, to improve your clinching skills, you may have your partner spar an inside fight while you attempt to muffle his attack and clinch as he attempts to stave off your clinch. Once the fight moves to the outside, you agree to bring the fight back to the inside range.

Sparring
Now all bets are off. You and your opponent are each trying to hone individual games while trying to best each other. It's the ultimate goal of the boxing game, but I cannot stress enough the necessity of moving through the previous five steps before considering the sixth step.

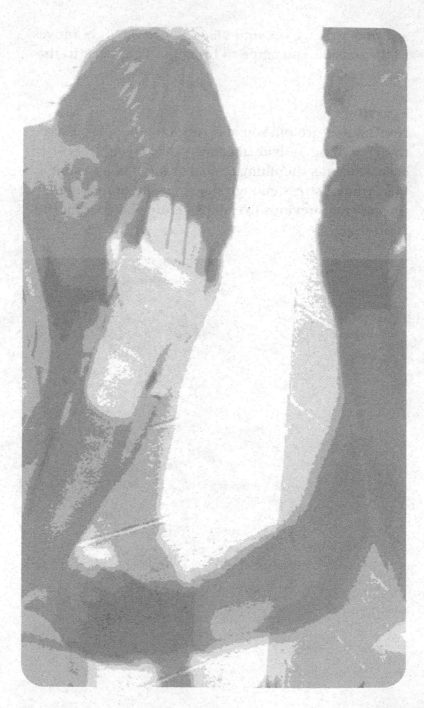

2 Stances and guards

It's not readily apparent, but there are varieties of stances in boxing. Each stance is or was designed to emphasize a particular offensive or defensive point or to make the most of a particular fighter's build. In this section, we will introduce six guards. Ideally, you will select the stance that feels best for you and work from there. I recommend a nodding familiarity with variations of your primary guard so that you can be effective if you find yourself faked into an awkward position or you choose to use an unorthodox guard to bait or confuse an opponent. My preference, the classic guard, will be used as the demonstration stance throughout this book, although the material will work with any of the guards presented.

Classic guard

● Picture yourself standing on a clock face. Left lead fighters stand with their left foot at 11 o'clock and their right foot at 4 o'clock. Right lead fighters stand with their right foot at 2 o'clock and their left foot at 8 o'clock.

● Your feet are approximately shoulder width apart with weight carried equally between the two feet.

● Your toes face forward with only the slightest inside turn of the toes of the lead foot.

● You feel your weight through the balls of your feet without actually being on your toes.

● Your knees are slightly bent for fluid movement.

● Hands are up.

● The rear fist touches the rear side of the jaw.

● The lead fist is held at the level of the lead shoulder, extended approximately one foot in front of that shoulder.

● Keep your elbows parallel and not flared into an inverted letter V.

● Keep your chin down toward the sternum.

● Keep your shoulders up for jaw protection.

● Noted proponents of the classic guard style were Gene Tunney and Sugar Ray Robinson.

Peekaboo guard
● This is a variation of the classic guard made famous by trainer Cus d'Amato and Floyd Patterson. Only the differences from the previous guard are addressed.

● The crouch is a bit deeper to shield more of the body.

● The parallel forearms are raised higher to better protect the head.

● The fists are left unclenched except when punching.

● Defense from the peekaboo guard is primarily shelling up and picking off incoming punches with slight inward and outward parries.

Crouch

● This is a peekaboo guard variant favored by aggressive body punchers.

● It is ideal for upstairs/downstairs punching.

● This is a strong stance for hooks and uppercuts but calls for lots of head movement and bobbing and weaving because the deeper stance makes swift footwork more difficult.

● To assume the stance, maintain the peekaboo hand position and widen the clock face, which lowers your body's center of gravity.

● This stance was used to great effect by Jack Dempsey, Tommy Burns and Mike Tyson (early career).

Jeffries crouch

● This crouch uses the widened clock face principle, but the hands are carried more forward than in the classic guard hand position.

● It is a good guard for short straight body punching and hooks to the body. Its limitations are reduced foot mobility and lack of head coverage.

● This stance is named for its major proponent, Jim Jeffries.

Philly shell

● This interesting guard variation calls for carrying the lead arm in a shoulder roll position. It is excellent for body protection and for delivering hooks. It is a somewhat poor guard from which to throw jabs.

● To assume the stance, turn your lead shoulder to face the opponent — toward noon on the clock face. Your rear hand moves to cover your lead jaw by placing the back of your rear hand against the lead jaw line. The lead arm is carried low with the glove covering the liver/solar plexus. The lead shoulder is carried high as additional jaw protection.

● This guard has been utilized to great effect by many great boxers from Philadelphia, notably Joe Frazier.

Cross guard
● This is essentially a hybrid between a crouch guard and a Philly shell.

● Assume the widened clock face position. Move the rear hand across your face as you do in the Philly shell. Then cross your lead glove to protect the rear jaw line. This hand position can be reversed with your rear forearm resting on the outside.

● Be aware that although this variation is an effective defensive guard for shelling up, the crossed arm position traps an arm rendering you unable to respond or initiate with optimum speed.

● This unusual guard was used to great effect by Freddie Mills and Len Harvey.

3 Footwork

This is a key skill often overlooked by many novices eager to get to the punching. Without solid footwork you will never reach your opponent with a firm base underneath your punches. Even more detrimental, you will be caught flat when receiving punches, and this is the surest way to lose a fight. I strongly advise you to pay attention to the footwork concepts provided and hone them with the accompanying drills.

● Maintain a shoulder-width stance even when moving. This is the only way to remain in balance.

● Resist the urge to bounce, hop or Ali shuffle with your steps. These excess movements waste energy that will be at a premium in later rounds. Flashy footwork also makes you light on the canvas removing solid support for your punches.

● Strive to keep your feet in contact with the floor at all times, even while stepping. Think step and drag at all times.

Step and drag forward.

Aligning with an opponent

It is also important to consider where your feet are placed in relation to your opponent's. Ideally, your lead foot is aimed between his legs. Many fighters move with their feet in line to their opponent's — a line can be drawn from the lead foot to the opponent's rear foot, and another line from the rear foot to the opponent's lead foot. They are positioned as if standing on the rails of a train track facing each other. This alignment gives each fighter similar offensive and defensive opportunities.

Step and drag outside (stepping latterly toward the lead).

Your goal is to take superior position by offsetting this alignment and placing your lead foot to the inside position. This removes your opponent's rear hand's offensive and defensive opportunities. Keep this in mind while drilling your footwork.

Step and drag
The step and drag is a specialized movement pattern vital to boxing success. It requires that you step in the direction you want to move with the foot that leads in that direction and then drag the trail foot to reestablish your ideal stance and guard.

Step and drag back 45 degrees left.

Work the following drills for at least one round each.

- Step and drag forward
- Step and drag retreat

● Step outside and drag — Stepping outside means stepping laterally toward your lead side. Left leads will step to their left, southpaws to their right.

● Step inside and drag — To step inside, left leads will step their right foot to the right and drag while southpaws will step the left foot to the left and drag.

- Step back 45 degrees left
- Step back 45 degrees right

● Speed retreat — This is essentially a step and drag retreat performed at top speed evading a pressing attack.

Step and drag speed retreat.

Pivoting inside.

Pivot

A pivot is a footwork maneuver that requires you to pivot on the ball of the lead foot to either direction and sweep/drag the rear foot around in the appropriate direction. Pivots can and should be combined with the above drills to create a fluid and preferably unpredictable movement style.

Pivoting drills

- Pivot inside
- Pivot outside

Centering

An important concept in ring generalship is to control the center of the ring. Your job is to keep your back off the ropes and turnbuckles and to maneuver your opponent so that his back is always relatively close to the ropes and turnbuckles. You do this by consciously being aware of getting yourself back to the center of the ring and pressuring him out of the center.

These centering drills will help seat this concept.

● Retreat and circle outside to return to the center.

● Retreat and circle inside to return to the center.

● Retreat/feint/circle outside back to center. To feint is to fake a punch. See Chapter 15.

● Retreat/feint/circle inside back to center.

● Retreat/feint/circle inside and then wheel outside. To wheel is to speedily change directions.

● Retreat/feint/circle outside/wheel inside.

Clapper

This drill will help build footwork reflexes. You will learn to switch directions at someone else's dictates rather than your own. I suggest working each step of it for several rounds until it is second nature.

To prepare for this drill, you must hang a small bean bag or any other light target (even a sheet of paper will do) in the center of the ring/training area. The target should be at chin height. You will stand approximately eight to ten feet away from the target.

Phase I — Begin circling clockwise. Your trainer will clap at random intervals. When you hear the clap, circle in the opposite direction.

Phase II — Each time the trainer claps twice, step forward and throw a jab at the target and then shuffle out to change directions.

Phase III — When the trainer claps three times, shuffle in and throw a jab/cross combination and then shuffle out to change directions.

Phase IV — When the trainer claps four times, step in and fire a jab/cross/lead hook and then shuffle out to change directions.

4 Upper body mobility

Footwork alone is not enough to make you a difficult target and to disguise your offensive intentions. You should strive to make the entire body slippery or hard to hit. To make this concept a reality, you must learn to marry crafty upper body movements with footwork drills. There are essentially two approaches to upper body mobility — long rhythm and short rhythm. You will likely find one more suitable to your style and body composition than the other, but it is integral that you work both since each serves a vital purpose in different fight contexts. Before tackling the two styles, keep the following rules in mind.

● The upper body is always in motion to reduce target acquisition and to make your offensive probes hard to read.

● The movements, whether long or short rhythm, are only one head width. Any movement more than that is wasted motion that can pull you out of good guard position.

● Take your hands with you as you move. It is a common error to move the head but leave the hands stationary making the head an easy target.

Long rhythm
This is a back-and-forth rocking of the upper body normally executed at the outside range. Think Muhammad Ali.

Short rhythm
This is a quick side to side movement performed as you move to the inside. For an excellent demonstration of short rhythm observe Joe Frazier.

Bobbing and weaving
Many people can envision a slick boxer executing a crafty bob and weave to escape and frustrate an opponent, and it is indeed a thing of beauty to witness when performed well. Despite the visceral attraction to this flashy mode of defense, I want to dissuade you from using this method. Bobbing and weaving wastes precious time and energy and may leave you open for uppercuts, hooks and overhands. In its stead, I recommend developing slipping, feinting and side-stepping footwork to the best of your ability. But if I can't persuade you to abandon this mode of upper body work, at least work it with a minimum of effort and movement. The following drill will help establish efficient bob and weave work.

Bob and weave drill
Standing in your guard, have your trainer place his lead hand on top of your lead shoulder. With his hand on top of your shoulder, begin several rounds of bobbing and weaving, moving only enough to clear his forearm with each pass.

Once you feel comfortable with this drill, have your partner fire slow motion punches at your head. Your mission, should you choose to accept it, is to continue bobbing and weaving with scrupulous economy of movement.

Long rhythm.

Short rhythm.

Bob and weave drill.

5 Fist rolling

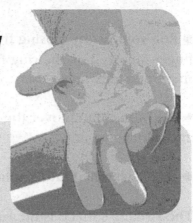

Yeah, I know. Been there, done that. Well, in order to be absolutely complete, let's be sure we really know what we're doing. There are 26 bones in the human hand, and boxers injure any number of these with enough frequency to have an ailment, "the boxer's fracture," named after them.

Here's how the old-timers of the bare-knuckle era made a fist when they were punching hard through up to 70 rounds.

● Roll your fist by closing from the outside in — little finger followed by the ring finger, middle finger and then the index finger.

● Fold your thumb over the middle joints of your index and middle fingers.

● You have rolled into a solid block.

The striking surface is the outside three knuckles (the middle, ring and little fingers), not the first two. Moreover, you shouldn't strike only with the top knuckles but with the entire three-finger surface area. By striking with the outside three fingers you are in proper skeletal alignment. All strikes will line up with the forearm's radius and ulna bones in a natural line that will prevent you from rolling and spraining your wrist.

It is advisable to learn to strike with the proper surface area in all drills, whether the target be training equipment, focus mitts or opponent. By proper fist rolling, focusing on the correct striking surface and proper hand protection, you will have done all you can to prevent hand injury.

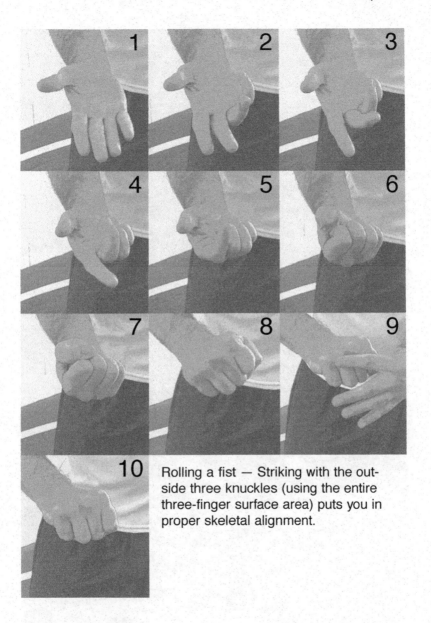

10 Rolling a fist — Striking with the outside three knuckles (using the entire three-finger surface area) puts you in proper skeletal alignment.

6 Hinge principle

There are two basic concepts that you should observe when throwing any punch. They are the hinge principle and the physics of power. Here, we will deal only with the former. For details on physics of power see *No Holds Barred Fighting: Savage Strikes* pages 15-19. The hinge principle is basically a physical analogy that teaches how to whip and snap every punch thus increasing range, speed, and above all, power.

The hinge principle requires you to imagine that your upper body is a door, the more solid the door the better. Your lead foot (more specifically, the ball of your lead foot) is the hinge of this heavy door. With each punch you throw, you are to imagine that you are slamming this door while pivoting sharply on this lead hinge. Let's look at a few basic punches and see how the hinge principle increases their effectiveness.

Jab
When executing the jab, you should slam the door toward the inside of your body (toward the direction your chest is facing) to fully exploit the range and power available with this weapon.

Cross/rear straight
With the cross, you will slam the door toward the outside of your body.

Lead hook
With the lead hook, you will slam the door to the inside.

Rear hook
Rear hooks require slamming the door to the outside of your body.

The hinge principle utilizes your entire body mass. Most people punch with only their arms and shoulders

or slam only with a waist twist. With the hinge principle, you deliver over the lead foot giving you the edge in power and reach.

Jab.

When consuming any information in this volume, do so with the tacit understanding that the hinge principle is always in play.

Cross.

Hinge principle

Lead hook.

Rear hook, profile.

7 Punches

Anyone with even a nodding familiarity with boxing can probably name the basic punches. Before we move on to combination work and advanced tactics, let's be sure that you are getting the most out of the fundamental blows.

Essentially, there are only six punches: jab, cross, lead and rear hooks, and the lead and rear upper-cuts. But you can subdivide these punches according to target level and double your arsenal number to twelve. By adding a few variations to the basic arsenal, you can raise your punch number even higher.

Before getting into the mechanics of each punch, there are a few broad considerations that apply to all punches.

● Always observe the hinge principle when using any technique.

● Maximize your stopping force by utilizing the physics of power.

● Exhale with every punch — preferably from the nose. This serves a fourfold purpose:

1. Forceful exhalations allow for greater muscle in the punch. Think of the power lifter exhaling forcefully as he moves the bar.

2. By exhaling, you release body tension allowing you to be stronger and more relaxed. These attributes allow you to put greater snap into your punches.

3. Boxing is a game of counterpunching. Eventually you will receive a punch as you perform your offensive move. The forced exhalation helps make the receipt of your opponent's blow easier.

4. Exhaling through the nose and not the mouth allows you to keep your mouth shut and clamped on to your mouthpiece. Breathing through the mouth or opening your mouth for any reason raises the potential for a broken jaw. Ken Norton caught Muhammad Ali with his mouth open in one of their bouts and the jaw fracture was a given.

● Make the negative (retraction) portion of your punch just as crisp as your positive motion. Lazy returns create a field day for counterpunchers.

● Return immediately to your guard position. Identify the arc, plane or path that each punch is to travel and endeavor to retreat along the same path.

● Observe the first step of the training continuum and shadowbox often. Shadowboxing prepares you for missing. You will miss far more than you will hit. Shadowboxing will teach you to return to good guard whether you have hit or missed.

● Last, but certainly not least, always keep your guard up and snap those punches.

High jab.

High jab
Throw this punch straight from your guard position
and return it along the same path.

Your palm will be facing downward at impact.
Aim low on the head, specifically, the nose, mouth and
chin. These are the same targets for crosses.

Low jab
To fire a punch to the body, it is vital to lower yourself
to target level in order to take full advantage of your
body mass and ensure good defensive coverage.

Punching at a downward angle reduces power and causes poor defensive posture.

To fire a low jab or cross, step in with the lead foot and bend at the knees and waist simultaneously.

High cross

Snap this punch straight from your rear guard position and return it along the same path. Your hand will be in a palm down position upon impact. Using the hinge principle, you will punch off the rear foot to power this punch. Drive with the ball of the rear foot. The heel can be raised from the floor but not the ball of the foot. Do not flare your heel to the outside. This golfer's swing stance takes your body out of alignment and forfeits power and drive.

Study rear straight artists such as Muhammad Ali, Willie Pep, Sugar Ray Robinson, Sugar Ray Leonard, Gene Tunney and Larry Holmes. Ali's cross was so crisp that he was able to fire it as a lead punch, which is not recommended for the majority of us.

Low cross
Fire this body shot with the same considerations given to the low jab, but your waist bend will be to the opposite side.

High lead hook

The lead arm remains in a fixed 90 degree angle with no push through at the end of the punch. Your fist will be held palm down for tight hooks and palm facing you for longer range hooks. Your targets for high lead

and rear hooks are the lower center side of the jaw or the temple. Some fighters find success hooking to the neck. Observe great hook artists such as Rocky Marciano, Joe Frazier, Joe Louis, Sugar Ray Leonard, Jack Dempsey and Mike Tyson.

High rear hook

Observe all the considerations for the high lead hook, but keep in mind that straight punches are excellent counters for rear hooks.

Rear hooks are slower and easier to read weapons than lead hooks, so the rear hook should be fired only in a finishing combination or when a seemingly safe opportunity presents itself.

Low lead hook.

Low lead hook

Use the same lowering of the base shown in straight body shots when delivering low hooks.

Excellent body hook targets are the ribs, particularly up and under the floating ribs. Think Roy Jones Jr.'s body shot knockout of Virgil Hill.

You can also cause damage by firing hooks at the heart and to the hips. Hooking to the inside and outside of the upper arms usually brings an opponent's hands down leaving his head open.

Low rear hook

The low lead hook principles apply but the danger of leading with rear hooks (page 53) is multiplied for low rear body hooks.

High lead uppercut
The uppercut is an inside fighting weapon.

To fire, lower the punching hand six to eight inches while turning your hand palm in.

Stand up and snap the punch through the target without winding up.

The jaw is the primary target of high uppercuts.

Keep in mind that uppercuts are dangerous punches to lead with. It is best to throw them behind jabs.

It is also advisable to move slightly to the opponent's outside when firing the lead uppercut to diminish his defensive and countering opportunities.

Look at uppercut masters such as Mike Tyson, Jack Sharkey, Kid Gavilan and Muhammad Ali for inspiration.

High lead uppercut.

Punches

High lead uppercut.

Low lead uppercut

All lead uppercut considerations are in play except the starting guard is lowered by bending at the knees, and the optimal target is the solar plexus.

High rear uppercut

You will execute by turning your rear shoulder toward your opponent and dipping it.

Do not alter your guard as you set up this punch because this telegraphs your intention.

Step in with your lead foot and slightly to your outside and drive the punch off the ball of your rear foot.

It is best with all uppercuts to have the knees bent a bit more than usual to provide additional power since the hinge principle is not a factor.

The high rear uppercut is used primarily to pull someone out of a crouch, which sets them up to receive either crosses or hooks.

High rear uppercut.

Punches

High rear uppercut.

Rear low uppercut

The mechanics for the high rear uppercut as well as the lowered base consideration discussed for the low lead uppercut are in play.

Corkscrew off jab.

Corkscrew straights

Corkscrew straights are fired off the jab or cross. These two straight punches are fired with proper jab or cross mechanics, but upon impact, twist the fist 180 degrees for added cutting potential.

This final twist comes from the shoulder and not the elbow or wrist.

In standard jabs and crosses, your palm is facing down at the point of impact. With the corkscrew, you twist your fist until the thumb is facing downward.

The corkscrew is primarily used to inflict a cut on your opponent's face or to exacerbate damage to a pre-existing cut. There is no need to train them as body shots.

Corkscrew off cross.

Lead shovel hook

The shovel hook is a powerful body shot that splits the difference between a body hook and a body uppercut. It's called a shovel hook because its upward 45 degree arc is similar to a shoveling motion, as if throwing dirt

over your opposite shoulder.

It is not a lead weapon and is used mainly inside. The heart, floating ribs and solar plexus are ideal targets for this punch.

Rear shovel hook

The rear shovel hook follows the mechanics of the lead shovel.

Rear shovel hook.

Kangaroo hook

This punch was used most effectively by Floyd Patterson and was developed by his trainer, Cus D'Amato.

It is useful against tall opponents but there are drawbacks. A fighter must travel a fair distance (outside to inside) and throw a rather looping punch that may be easily blocked or countered.

It is essentially a long lead hook accompanied by a forward shuffling jump into your opponent.

You should crouch in your guard at the outside range before firing.

Fire this punch with maximum speed to compensate for its previously mentioned deficiencies that telegraph intention.

Kangaroo hook.

Punches

Bolo.

Bolo punch
A bolo has little use in a legitimate boxing arsenal, but since you see them occasionally, we will discuss them.

A bolo is little more than a flashy uppercut that depends upon speed and carries little power. It is first and foremost a showboat move.

To throw a bolo, whip your rear hand in a backward circle allowing it to snap up into your opponent's chin.

Depending on your sources, bolos were first thrown by either Kid McCoy or ex-middleweight champ Cefarino Garcia. They have been used by many fighters since including Sugar Ray Leonard and Roy Jones Jr. Bolos were used to their best effect by Cuban welterweight Kid Gavilan.

8 KOs and power punching

Everyone loves KOs. You can win a fight by decision and be beautiful while you do it, but there is no denying the visceral appeal of the decisive knockout. True boxing artistry does not require you to have a KO to your name to be a champion. But there's no harm in trying. We will discuss a few of the aspects beyond the physics of power to get you closer to this elusive but powerful skill.

Contrary to popular belief, the most essential attribute needed to become a KO artist is not power (although it's certainly nice to have). It's more important to have range mastery, accuracy, timing and speed.

Knockout punching is not about loading up and looking for a Sunday punch. Instead it is boxing well — knowing where, when and how to hit. And even then, the deciding factors seem to be the ability and desire to hit often — not just hard.

Realize that form is more important than power and strength. Strive for perfect form. Once that is attained, efficiency of movement will allow speed to follow naturally. Then form and speed will combine to create power. The key to making this formula work is repetition, repetition, repetition.

It is essential that you identify the optimum range of each punch in your arsenal and throw the proper punch at the proper time. For example, there is no denying that uppercuts are powerful weapons, but this is true only in an inside fight. At outside or even middle-ranges, they are useless. In other words, know which punch goes where.

Tight shovel hooks are responsible for more KOs than any other body shot. With that in mind, work them diligently and throw them when the opportunity presents itself.

It has been observed that knockouts "need room." That is, tight inside fighting is good for softening up the body, but the majority of knockout punches observed in bout after bout travel a minimum of 18 to 24 inches.

Sports physiologists inform us that muscles contract more forcefully if they are stretched before they contract. It is this stretch/contraction principle that creates the majority of plyometric conditioning programs. To observe this elastic/contraction phenomenon in bold relief, look to baseball. The pitcher winds up his pitch before the major contraction to assist in the power transference. The same holds true in batting.

Without the wind up the pitcher or batter relying on only brute strength will see little return. Examine your punching technique and realize that the hinge principle allows you to take full advantage of the elastic/contraction basis of power without sacrificing good guard.

Work with the elastic/contraction concept in mind but don't wind up every punch in an exaggerated manner. Use smaller motions to remain safe. Learn to embody the advice of Bob Fitzsimmons who said, "Hit from where your hand is."

Combinations result in KOs more than the solitary Sunday punch. Don't just stalk your man looking for the right time to throw a bomb. Box your opponent. Probe. Throw punches in combinations. An increase in punches increases the potential for a knockout.

Strive for pinpoint accuracy in training so you can hit the optimum knockout targets in bouts. There are spots on the human body conducive to KOs. If you cannot hit them, all this information is for naught. I highly recommend using focus mitts with target dots on them. Aim for the dot in the center of the mitt rather than anywhere on the mitt surface. You can mark a heavy bag with duct tape to practice accuracy as well as power. The difference between a good punch and a knockout is often a matter of inches in punch placement. Learn to be a sharpshooter.

● The best KO targets on the head are the temple and jaw, particularly the chin. Punching to the eye can close the eye or distract while you hit a follow-up shot.

Punching to the nose also can be used in this distraction/setup manner. Punching to the ears is another particularly annoying tactic and can be used successfully as setups.

● Excellent body shot targets are the solar plexus, the floating ribs, the heart (high on the left side) and the liver (low on the right side).

● The best body shot weapons are crosses, shovel hooks and uppercuts.

● Don't get hung up on this piece of advice — just absorb it and let the information float around in your skull. Try to time your body shots to connect when your opponent is inhaling. While taking a breath the abdominal musculature has to relax making impact more difficult to take. With experience you will be able to monitor your opponent's breathing rate and make the most of this tip.

● To flog a dead horse, don't wait for the perfect punch. That punch does not exist. Hit often and hit precisely. When you have an opportunity to punch, deliver it. Do not wait. Do not hesitate.

● Although it's important to hit often, do not flail. Do not swing wildly. Always hit with proper form and return to good guard.

● The objectives in boxing should be perfection of form, relaxation of the body and mind, complete control of your emotions and authority in the ring. Don't

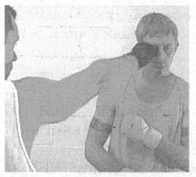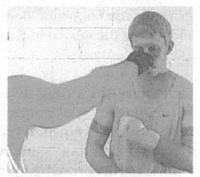

Eye and nose shots distract and serve as excellent setups.

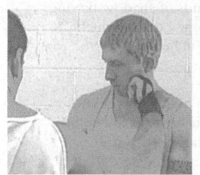

Power punches to the jaw and chin are prime KO targets.

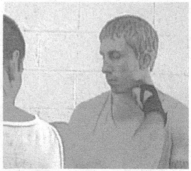

Temple shots yield KOs and throat punches disable and distract.

strive for the knockout. Be the best boxer you can be and follow the advice in this section. Knockouts may follow accordingly.

Jack Dempsey's cage drill

The explosive Jack Dempsey used this drill to build power. He was known to train in a ring (cage) that had a five-foot high roof (some reports list the height at four feet). This prevented him from standing at full height. You can forego the expense of building such a cage by working several rounds of shadow boxing, focus mitts and heavy bag from a deep crouch. Do not allow yourself to stretch to full height until the round is over.

Working from a deep crouch builds power and endurance in the legs and teaches you to explode though punches. I heartily endorse this drill.

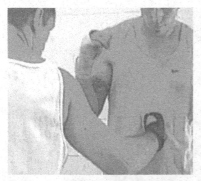 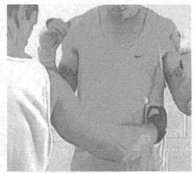

Body targets include the solar plexus, the floating ribs ...

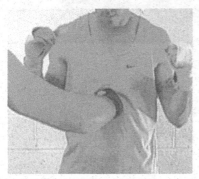 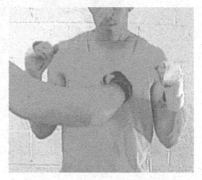

... the liver and heart.

9 Jab drills

Jab is king.

It is the most used and most valued punch for good reason. The jab is your probe — it allows you to test your opponent to see  what sort of defense he has. The jab is your range finder — telling you when you need to move or fire a follow-up punch. The jab is your best defensive weapon — moving behind a stiff jab can keep an opponent at bay. The jab is the premier tool to set up all other punches. In short, the jab is the best friend you have in boxing. Learn it well.

Several jab drills and varieties of jabs to add to your arsenal follow. While working these drills, remember to observe all of the proper mechanics of throwing a jab. To aid in your education, look to masters such as Muhammad Ali, Sugar Ray Robinson, Sugar Ray Leonard, Tommy Loughran, Tommy Hearns, Larry Holmes and Willie Pep.

Hitting on the fly

Hitting on the fly is simply moving after you throw a punch. Seldom (if ever) will you stay put in your footwork or upper body rhythm after you throw a punch. Movement is key to good boxing. The following drills will help seat that skill. I recommend working several rounds of each.

- Jab and advance
- Jab and retreat
- Jab and move left
- Jab and move right
- Jab and move clockwise
- Jab and move counterclockwise

1-6 Jab and advance.

1-6 Jab and move right.

1-8 Jab and move clockwise.

Multiples and levels

The jab can (and often should) be thrown in combinations. It is also wise to change levels with multiple jabs to work both body and head.

Key Point — If the last punch you throw in a combination is to the body, you need to move out immediately because you are open for countering. You can open

Photos 1-14
Jab the head,
jab the body
and retreat.

with and insert a body shot in the middle of a combination, but don't finish with a body shot without retreating fast and with good guard.

Once you've worked the drill suggestions on the next two pages for several rounds, come up with your own multiples.

Double jab to the head.

Jab the body, jab the head.

Double jab the head, jab the body and retreat.

- Double jab to the head

  Jab the head, jab the body and retreat

  Jab the body, jab the head

- Triple jab the head

  Double jab the head, jab the body and retreat

  Jab the head, double jab the body and retreat

  Jab the head, jab the body, jab the head

  Jab the body, jab the head, jab the body and retreat

  Quadruple jab the head

  Jab the head, triple jab the body and retreat

  Double jab the head, double jab the body and retreat

- Triple jab the head, jab the body and retreat

- Jab the body, triple jab the head

- Double jab the body, double jab the head

- Triple jab the body, jab the head

Lead jolt.

Jab varieties

The jab is not only the most useful of punches, it's also the most versatile. Beyond the standard classic jab and the corkscrew variation already covered, there are at least five other jab varieties to be familiar with. Each has specific uses.

Lead jolt

Jack Dempsey used this variety of jab to increase his power. To fire, observe all of the standard mechanics but step forward forcefully with a hard step timing the impact of your punch with the foot's impact on the canvas. The step is an exaggerated stomp.

Lunge jab.

Lunge jab

This jab is used to cover a great deal of distance. Use a longer step than in the lead jolt, but the stomp is not exaggerated. Think the long lunge used in fencing.

Speed or show jab

The speed jab (above) is all arm with no hinge. To fire, take your fist straight from its on-guard position directly to the target. There should be no telegraphing whatsoever from any other portion of the body.

Pivot jab.

Post jab.

Pivot jab

This jab is used to get you from outside to inside range and act as a cover at the same time. To fire, throw your jab and rotate the jab shoulder inward toward your jaw to provide cover against incoming counters. Move in behind this jab to establish an inside fight.

Post jab

This is another offensive/defensive combination. Fire the jab and upon impact leave it at full extension. This is essentially a post and should muffle his counters.

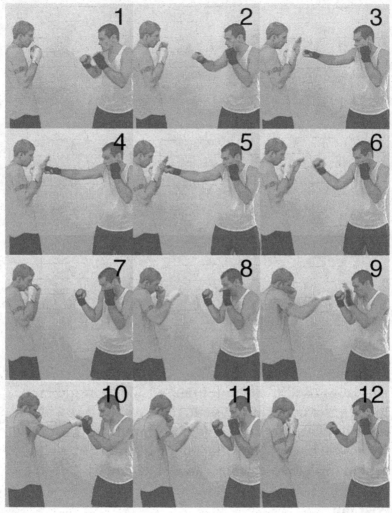

Jab and catch.

Jab and block drills
Jabs are usually countered with a return jab, a cross or
a lead hook. The following drills will hone your
answers to these common responses.

Jab and catch

Throw a jab to the head. Your partner immediately will
return a jab to your head. Catch his jab in the open
palm of your rear hand.

Jab and cover

You throw a jab and your partner returns a lead hook.
Cover your rear ear with the glove of your rear hand,
bend your knees and bend slightly forward at the waist
to block the hook.

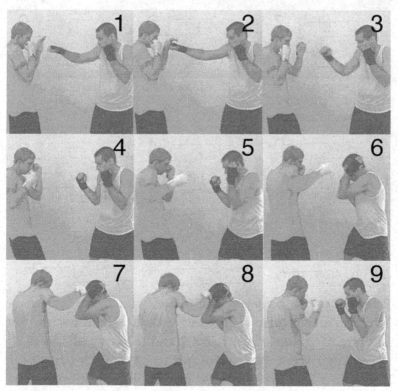

Jab and cover.

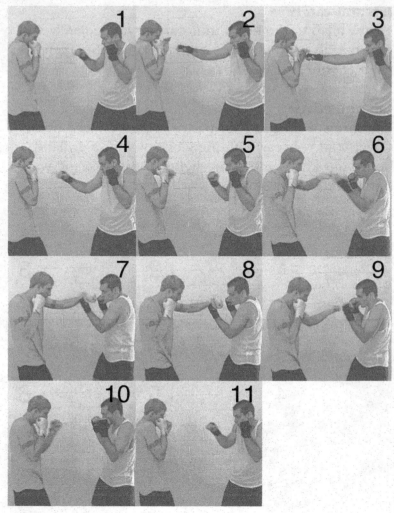

Jab and cross parry.

Jab and cross parry

Your partner returns a cross to your head after your jab. Use the palm of your rear hand to parry his cross at his inner wrist. Be careful not to cross your centerline with your parry. Provide just enough motion to redirect his punch.

Low guard jabs

It is common to see jabs fired from the lead arm held either across the liver or at waist level. Throwing from a low guard position is not recommended. It is preferable to throw the jab from a high guard, but there will be times when you are out of position or using an unorthodox strategy. Make sure that you return the punching hand to high guard to cover counter openings.

Work jabs from the liver and belt levels.

Jab from the liver.

Jab from the belt.

Sway jab
The lead arm dangles and rocks in a slight pendulum motion at the beltline. Practice firing the jab straight out of this swaying motion.

Low jab
Jabs to the body are underutilized by most boxers. I recommend you become as proficient jabbing to the body as you are with head hunting. Keep in mind that once you jab to the body you've got to exit immediately since bending at the waist puts you in danger of counters. Move out low and fast.

Sway jab.

The drills on the following three pages will develop the movement necessary to become a low jab artist.

● Low jab and step-out
● Low jab, step to the inside
● Low jab, step to the outside

Jab drills

Low jab and step out.

Low jab, step to the inside.

Low jab, step to the outside.

Low jab and high hook ... more next page.

Low jab and high lead hook

Placing a second punch high allows you to break the exit low rule. Jab low, immediately follow with a high lead hook. Then wheel quickly to the inside to foil counters.

10 Combinations

It's time to put the single punches together into combinations. Combinations are key to boxing mastery. In this section you will find many combinations but not all the possible permutations by any stretch of the imagination. By developing the ones provided to the best of your ability and utilizing linked combinations (page 123) and beat punching (Chapter 11) you will have hours and hours of material to hone.

Before we get to the combinations, here are a few considerations.

● Throw in combination whenever possible. Combinations confuse your opponent and increase your odds of victory.

● Think "up and down" or "vice versa" in combinations. In other words, set up body shots with head punches and set up blows to the head with body punches.

● When executing any combination, keep in mind that the best punch sequences flow from natural, synchronized movements of the body. Make optimum use of the hinge principle while maintaining good balance.

● It is ideal to finish combinations with a lead arm punch. This allows you to establish good balance and better able to counter your opponent's follow-ups.

● Mix it up. Mix straight punches with hooks and uppercuts. Use angles to confuse your opponent. Straight punches cause your opponent to narrow his guard opening him up for hooks. Hooks cause an opponent to widen his guard for straight punch targets. Uppercuts cause boxers to lower their guard for head hunting.

To summarize:
1. Use straight punches to set up hooks.
2. Use hooks to set up straight punches.
3. Use uppercuts to set up head shots.

● Combinations work because of the force of number. Commit the following Sugar Ray Robinson quote to memory, "I was really a weak puncher. It's the punch that you don't see coming that hurts."

● When working the following combination drills, don't forget the combinations included in the Jab Drills chapter. Unless a target is specified, body or head, assume each punch is fired to the head.

Two-punch combinations

1 Jab
2 Cross

1 Jab
2 Cross body

1 Jab body
2 Cross

1 Jab body
2 Cross body

Combinations

1 Jab	2 Lead hook
1 Jab	2 Lead uppercut
1 Cross	2 Lead hook
1 Cross	2 Lead hook body

When double-hooking, drop the lead hand to a 45 degree angle after the first hook. This gains a bit of distance for the second hook.

1 Lead hook body **2** Lead hook

1 Rear hook body **2** Rear hook

1 Rear uppercut **2** Lead hook

1 Rear uppercut **2** Cross

1 Rear uppercut   **2** Jab

Three-punch combinations

1 Jab   **2** Jab   **3** Cross

1 Jab   **2** Jab body   **3** Cross

Four-punch combinations

1 Jab

2 Cross

3 Lead hook body

4 Rear uppercut

1 Cross

2 Lead hook

3 Cross

4 Lead hook body

1 Jab

2 Lead hook body

3 Lead hook

4 Rear uppercut

1 Jab

2 Cross body

3 Lead hook

4 Rear hook body

Combinations

1. Lead uppercut
2. Rear hook
3. Lead hook body

4. Rear hook body

Five-punch combinations

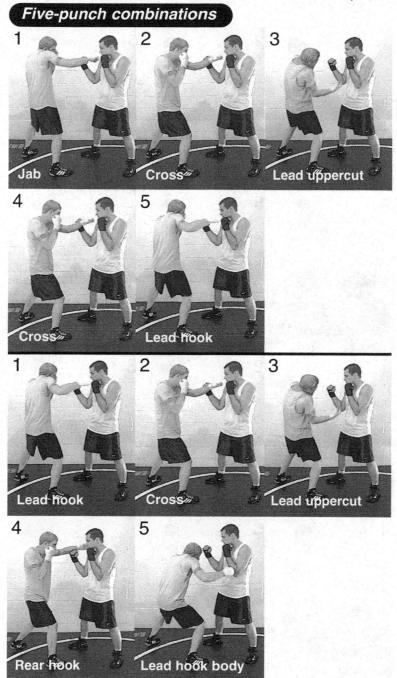

1 Jab

2 Cross

3 Lead uppercut

4 Cross

5 Lead hook

1 Lead hook

2 Cross

3 Lead uppercut

4 Rear hook

5 Lead hook body

Combinations

1 Jab

2 Cross

3 Lead hook

4 Lead hook

5 Cross

Doubling the lead hook can be quite useful against a shelled-up opponent.

1 Jab

2 Jab

3 Cross

4 Lead hook

5 Cross

Six-punch combinations

1 Jab
2 Cross
3 Lead hook
4 Cross
5 Lead uppercut
6 Rear uppercut

1 Jab
2 Cross
3 Lead uppercut
4 Cross
5 Lead hook
6 Rear uppercut

Combinations

1 Jab   2 Cross   3 Lead hook

4 Cross   5 Lead uppercut   6 Cross

Linking combinations

To create higher punch counts, learn to link small combinations. For example, a three-punch combo followed by a two-punch combo followed by another three-punch combo equals eight punches thrown in sequence.

In this manner you can mix and match offensive combinations 15-20 punches deep without having to memorize high number combos. Linking combinations allows you to take the finite number of combinations provided and exponentially raise the variations in your attack.

Work these linked combinations with no break in the internal portion of each smaller unit and with only a slight regrouping or pause between the differing sets. In the drills the dash (—) represents a pause.

● Jab — Jab, rear uppercut — jab, rear uppercut, lead hook — jab, rear uppercut, hook, cross

● Cross — cross, lead uppercut — cross, lead uppercut, lead hook

● Jab — jab, lead hook — jab, cross, lead hook — jab, cross, lead uppercut, cross, hook

● Jab — jab, rear uppercut — jab, jab, cross

11 Beat punching

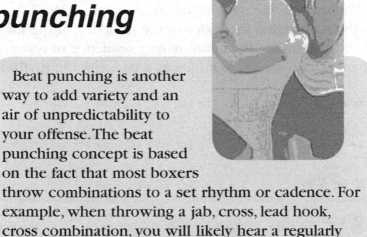

Beat punching is another way to add variety and an air of unpredictability to your offense. The beat punching concept is based on the fact that most boxers throw combinations to a set rhythm or cadence. For example, when throwing a jab, cross, lead hook, cross combination, you will likely hear a regularly timed 1 2 3 4 beat on the heavy bag or focus mitts.

Since most fighters train in specific cadences, the tendency is to expect incoming punches to follow specific cadences as well. By training yourself to break your natural cadence and introduce a variety of punch rhythms, you will confuse and upset your opponent's defensive timing and composure. You can take the concept of beat punching and apply it to any of the already listed combinations or to any linked set of combinations. The following set of drills will illustrate how to apply the beat concept to any combination work.

If we take a standard four-punch combination and number each punch 1 2 3 4, we can manipulate these numbers to come up with entirely new animals without changing the order of the punches. In the following examples, the combination sequence never changes. The dash (—) indicates a pause in the rhythm.

1 2 3 4

1 — 2 3 4

1 2 — 3 4

1 2 3 — 4

1 — 2 — 3 4

1 — 2 3 — 4

We have taken a standard combination (1 2 3 4) through five variations. It may not seem like much of a revelation on the page, but I strongly encourage you to work this concept in the gym. You will find it pays off rather quickly. By observing and utilizing these rhythm breaks, you lift yourself from the rank of journeyman puncher to the realm of slick technician.

12
Defensive concepts

Novice boxers and average boxing fans admire punching ability. Expert boxers and informed fans admire defensive skill. Successful boxing is a game of giving more than you receive. Be mindful of these bits of wisdom as you practice.

● The great Rocky Marciano (an unlikely source for boxing defense) said, "The best fighters hit the most and get hit the least."

● Boxing is 50% offense and 50% defense.

● Boxing's 80/20 rule says that your lead hand will perform 80% of the offense and 20% of the defense. Your rear hand does 80% of the defense and 20% of the offense.

● Keep your eyes on your opponent.

● Keep your chin down.

● Keep your mouth closed.

● Keep moving when you are in punching range — use long or short rhythm or both.

● Don't lunge with your punches.

● After a punch or defensive motion, immediately return to guard.

● Don't give as much as you take — give more than you take.

● Don't lean back to avoid punches. Doing so leaves you with nothing to follow up with or with no place to go if your opponent is pressing the attack.

● Don't use both hands to block a single punch. Using two hands leaves more of your body open and rules out the possibility of counterpunching.

● Blocking is performed close to the body or face.

● Don't reach out to intercept or block punches. Doing so places you in an unguarded position.

● When you get hit (and you will get hit), don't get angry. Stay composed, stay on your game and get to work.

● Observe the great defensive artists for inspiration. They include fighters such as Muhammad Ali, Willie Pep, Sugar Ray Leonard, Joe Frazier, Sugar Ray Robinson, Pernell Whitaker and Wilfredo Benitez.

13
Defense
mechanics

As with all the material, work each individual element in isolation rounds to hone a feel for the technique. Once this is done attempt limited sparring to begin learning where and when each described defense is used.

Catching a jab.

Cuffing a jab.

High jab defenses

● **Catch**
Allow the punch to land in the palm of your rear glove approximately 8-12 inches in front of your face.

Do not smack the punch down because this opens you up for counters. However, it is advisable to smack the punch up slightly upon impact.

● **Cuff**
Smack at the outer wrist of your opponent's jab arm with the palm of your rear hand. Do not allow your cuffing arm to travel across your chest.

Draw a small circle with the cuff hand. Circle back toward your chest after impacting your opponent's wrist rather than across your body.

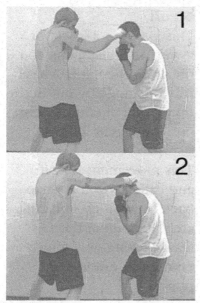

Inside slip away from a jab.

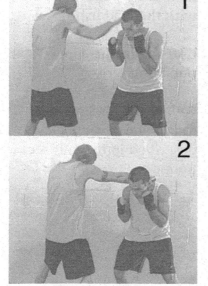

Outside slip away from a jab.

● **Inside slip**

Lean your upper body slightly lateral to the inside of your opponent's punch (the inside is toward his chest).

The movement should be just enough for the punch to miss — no more, no less.

Keep in mind that anytime you slip inside a punch, you are in danger of being struck by your opponent's opposite hand. Stay alert.

● **Outside slip**

The reverse of the inside slip.

Perform a slight lateral lean to the outside of your opponent's punch (toward his back).

● Pull

This is called a "rock" or "sway" in some gyms. You break momentarily a basic rule of stance by putting up to 70% of your weight onto your rear foot.

This movement is swift and calls for you to snap back to position immediately. Remain in the leaning state only long enough to evade the punch.

Pulling back from a jab.

● Cross glove

Essentially perform a cuff with the lead hand.

Cuff against his inner punching wrist.

Follow the circling back to the chest mechanics described in the cuff section.

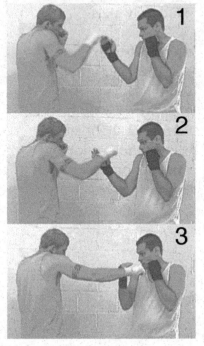

Cross glove against a jab.

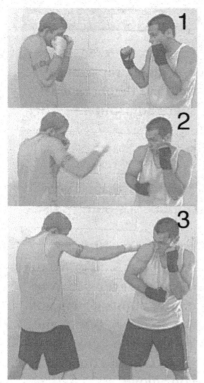

● Shoulder roll and shoulder block

Drop your lead glove across your liver and turn your lead shoulder toward the punch.

Be sure to keep your chin down and your shoulder raised high. Allow the punch to land on the deltoid mass of your shoulder.

● Step back

Driving off your lead foot, step and drag quickly in retreat just out of the punch's range.

Shoulder blocking a jab.

Stepping back from a jab.

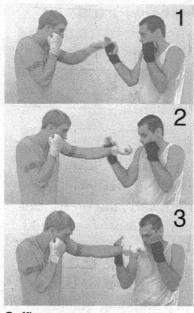

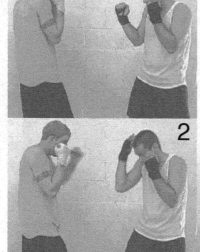

Cuffing a cross.

High cross defenses

High cross defenses are essentially the same as high jab defenses with slight adjustments.

● Cuff

You will cuff with the lead hand against your opponent's outer wrist.

● Cover or block

Raise your lead glove to cover your temple. Your elbow points down, not out. Bend slightly at the knees and receive the punch on the outside of your glove.

Blocking a cross.

- **Inside slip**
- **Outside slip**
- **Pull or rock**
- **Cross glove**

Use your rear hand to cuff your opponent's cross.

Slipping inside (top) and outside from a cross.

Rocking back from a cross.

Cross glove against a cross.

Defense mechanics

Shoulder roll against a cross.

Stepping back from a cross.

Blocking a high hook.

- **Shoulder roll**

- **Step back**

High lead hook defenses

- **Cover**
Bring your rear glove over your temple with your elbow pointing down.

Bend at the knees and forward at the waist to cut angle off the punch.

136

● Duck

The ducking pattern describes the letter V.

Bend at the knees and forward at the waist as you duck forward at a 45 degree angle. Rise at a 45 degree angle into your opponent.

Remember, you must bend at the knees as well as the waist. Bending only at the waist causes these three mishaps:

1. Your eyes will be directed at the floor and not your opponent.

2. You will be temporarily immobile and unbalanced.

3. You will be out of position for countering.

By bending at the knees and keeping your eyes on your opponent, you are ready to defend and counter intelligently.

Ducking a high hook.

Pulling back from a lead hook.

● **Pull**

● **Cross glove**
A cross glove versus a hook is different from the cross glove used against straight punches.

It is basically a variant of a catch.

Here, the palm of your lead glove seeks to smack directly into the fist of the incoming hook.

Rock the upper body back just enough to make the punch miss.

● **Step back**

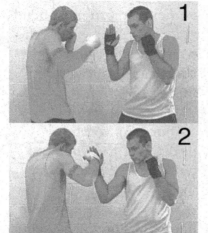

Cross glove against a lead hook.

Stepping back from a lead hook.

Covering against a rear hook.

High rear hook defenses

- **Cover**
- **Duck**
- **Pull**
- **Cross glove**
- **Step back**

Ducking a rear hook.

Cross glove against a rear hook.

Pulling back from a rear hook.

Stepping back from a rear hook.

Forearm block against an uppercut.

Uppercut / shovel hook defenses

● **Forearm block**
Receive the lead or rear punch on either forearm.

Turn the blocking side of your torso slightly toward the punch so that the forearm block provides full coverage.

Block right uppercuts and shovels with your left forearm and left uppercuts and shovels with your right forearm. This is optimum, although either forearm ca be used.

Glove block against an uppercut.

● **Glove block**
To glove block an uppercut or shovel, use right glove versus right punch and vice versa.

Smack the palm of your glove downward into the incoming fist.

● **Pull**
● **Step back**

Pulling back from an uppercut.

Stepping back from an uppercut.

1

2

3

Scooping a low jab.

Low jab defenses

● Scoop

A scoop can be performed with either the lead or rear hand. The rear hand is preferable because you can counter with the lead.

Think of your elbow remaining in position on a ball and socket joint and your hand traveling in a downward arc to parry/scoop the incoming blow to the outside of your body.

● Forearm block
● Step back

Forearm blocking low jab.

Stepping back from a low jab.

Scooping a low cross.

Forearm blocking a low cross.

Stepping back from a low cross.

Low cross defenses

- **Scoop**
- **Forearm block**
- **Step back**

Forearm blocking a low hook.

Low hook defenses

- **Forearm block**
- **Step back**

Stepping back from a low hook.

14 Isolation and touch sparring

To hone your offensive and defensive games, I recommend isolation and touch boxing.

Isolation sparring

An isolation boxing drill is sparring with a limited, agreed upon arsenal. Only specific punches are thrown so that boxing partners can work and hone those punches and the appropriate defenses for each. Since the boxing is limited and specific, egos are left outside the ring in order to focus on skill development.

Following are a few isolation drills to get you started. Work each for several rounds applying variety to your defense. Always work on timing. Play with lighter contact in a tit for tat manner, meaning that you throw and then your partner throws. Even though the punches and order of attack are predetermined, strive to control the match with timing, pace and footwork.

● Jab for jab

● Cross for cross

● Jab/cross for jab/cross

- Lead hook for lead hook

- Rear hook for rear hook

- Lead uppercut for lead uppercut

- Rear uppercut for rear uppercut

Touch boxing

Touch boxing is another excellent drill that highlights defensive training without hard contact. Hard hitting takes you back to old, ineffective patterns of response. Here you are allowed to throw any punch in any combination in no pre-set order. But this must be accomplished at a designated pace dictated by your trainer, and all contact must be light.

You can call out percentages of contact and speed before each round. For example, 100% is an all out match at maximum speed and contact.

Contact percentages should range from 10% to 30%, but speed can be as low as 10% and as high as 100%. Remember, because contact is light, speed does not have to be abandoned. Just as with isolation boxing, you are striving to develop specific attributes.

The safe confines of these two drills allow you to explore offensive and defensive areas that even friendly sparring matches don't permit.

15 Feinting

Feinting is the art of the fakeout. It's trickery and deception. A feint is any false offensive movement used to draw a response from your opponent that causes him to pull himself out of good defensive position leaving him open for your real attack.

Here are few tips on feints and a dozen feinting drills to master this skill.

Master the "look off"
● Most people instinctively watch the eyes to determine offensive intentions. Look at the body and the opponent will expect a body shot; look at his jaw and he'll expect a head shot. Don't look at what you want to hit ... fake him out.

● When a feint doesn't draw a punch, always come back with a jab so that no motion is wasted.

● Slow your punching speed or change the pace of your footwork. Either will surprise your opponent and allows you to accelerate once a response is elicited.

● The most successful feints use the eyes, hands, torso and legs in concert.

Arm Feints
Appear to punch a certain area with a hand and then quickly shift to another target.

Body Feints
Make sudden body moves such as advancing quickly, dropping the knees or pivoting shoulders to check your opponent's reaction.

Masters of the feint include Muhammad Ali, Sugar Ray Robinson, Sugar Ray Leonard, Willie Pep and Benny Leonard. The latter is often credited with having invented this art.

Feint drills
The following drills are only a few of the many possible feints. By working each for several rounds and implementing them in your sparring, multiple variations will present themselves. The dashes (—) represent pauses between combination sets.

Feint low, jab high, retreat.

Feinting

Feint high, jab low, retreat.

Jab, retreat — feint, retreat — feint, jab high.

Jab, cross, retreat — feint, retreat — feint, jab, cross.

Jab, rear hook, retreat — feint, retreat — feint, jab, rear hook.

Feint a low jab, lead hook high.

Feint a high jab, lead hook.

Feint a low jab, cross head.

Feint the jab, cross.

Feint the cross, lead hook.

Lead shoulder feint, cross.

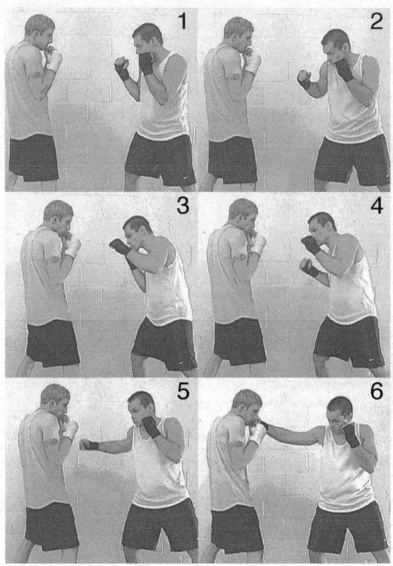

Lead shoulder feint, feint the cross, lead hook.

16 Drawing

Drawing is the opposite of feinting. In feinting you use a false offensive action to bait your opponent out of position. In drawing you expose defensive flaws that will tempt him to attack. In other words, you use drawing to make the opponent come to you. You will leave the head or body unprotected to draw a particular attack that you are ready to counter.

There is also a difference in attitude between feinting and drawing. Feinting is aggressive because you provoke a desired response. Drawing passively dangles the bait as your opponent is lured into action.

But drawing and feinting both benefit from the "triple," which is a pattern used to "teach" your opponent what you want him to do or expect. For example, you may feint a jab to the head and return to a lazy guard twice, allowing your opponent to see your "mistake." The third time you do it, your opponent will usually choose to capitalize upon your "error." This is when you spring your drawing or feinting trap.

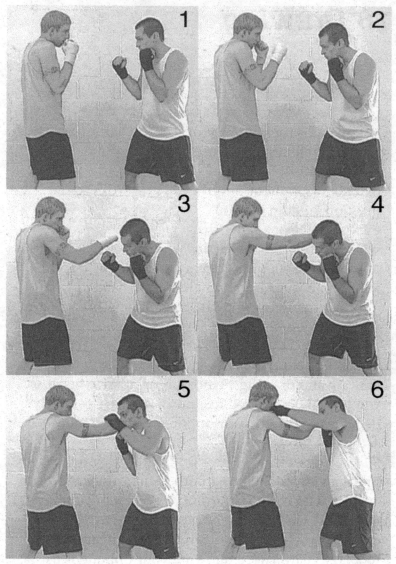

Move your head forward a few inches to draw a jab, slip outside and return a cross.

Use the head to invite the jab, slip outside and return a lead hook.

Lower the lead hand to invite a cross, catch it when it is fired and return a lead hook.

Lower the lead hand to invite a cross, catch it and fire a lead uppercut.

Drawing

Lower the lead hand to invite a cross, slip inside and throw a lead hook.

Invite a cross, slip inside and deliver a lead hook body, cross head, lead hook head.

Drawing

Raise the lead hand to invite a cross to the body, drop the lead elbow to block and jab head.

Raise the lead hand to invite a cross to the body, drop the elbow to defend and cross head.

Drawing

Draw a lead hook by lowering your rear hand, move inside his hook and lead hook head.

Draw a lead hook, move inside and lead uppercut head.

Draw a lead hook, move inside, lead shovel hook.

Jab, retreat, jab, retreat, jab — and when your opponent follows your retreat — connect with another jab ...

... or fire a cross ...

... or step to his outside and throw hooks to the body and head.

17 Pivoting and waltzing

These two tactics are specific footwork methods used when an opponent is coming to you. With both the pivot or the waltz, you are re-directing your body mass.

The pivot is covered in chapter 3. Here we add a few punches to highlight its importance. If you recall, a pivot is stepping back with your rear foot in a wide sweep toward your outside (your back) while you pivot smoothly on the ball of the lead foot. To gain the maximum countering benefits from the pivot, work the following drills for several rounds. Have your training partner rush into you with a furious attack (see next two pages).

● Partner rushes in — pivot, cross head

● Partner rushes in — pivot, lead hook head

● Partner rushes in — pivot, cross head, lead hook head, cross head

Pivot, cross head.

After a pivot throw a lead hook head.

After a pivot fire a cross head, lead hook head, cross head.

Waltzing an opponent.

After waltzing him around throw crosses and lead hooks.

Waltzing is a pivot variant made famous by the graceful light heavyweight Georges Carpentier. The waltz is essentially a pivot combined with a side step to the outside.

Feint the lead hand and retreat drawing your opponent to come after you. As he steps in, step to your outside on your lead foot and then pivot on the ball of that foot. You may use your lead hand on your opponent's back, shoulder or arm to assist moving him by you.

Follow with any of the punch combinations used in this chapter.

There is a final step to Carpentier's waltz that is illegal. Once the waltz step has been performed, Carpentier would grab his opponent's lead shoulder with his lead hand, spin him back around and hit him with a rear hook (below).

18 Shifting

A shift is another footwork tactic that is used to either change leads as you retreat or advance. Shifting is changing your stance by stepping a rear foot to the lead or a lead foot to the rear. The step and drag should be your primary advancing and retreating weapon, but there are times when the shift is faster and allows you to add power to punches (particularly hooks and shovel hooks). The following drills will help you develop your shifting skills.

● Retreat shift — shift lead foot to rear

● Advance shift — shift rear foot to lead

● Retreat shift — fire a "lead" hook to the body (the former rear hand is now the lead hand and fires the hook)

● Advance shift — fire a "lead" hook to the body

● Retreat shift — fire a "lead" double hook (hook body, hook head)

● Advance shift — fire a "lead" double hook

Retreat shift, hook body, hook head.

Advance shift, hook body, hook head.

19 Shuffling: cutting off the ring, pressuring and cornering

Shuffling is yet another footwork tactic. Whereas the pivot, waltz and shift are primarily countering and defensive tools, the shuffle is almost always used offensively.

Shuffling is a side to side stepping used to follow an opponent who is caught on the ropes or to cut off the ring. You remain almost squared in your stance so that you can fire either hand. Following are drills to get you comfortable with this concept.

Shuffling

Cutting off the ring.

Cutting off the ring

Start in the center of the ring with a training partner. Use footwork to maneuver him against the ropes or into a corner. Use primarily side to side shuffling to accomplish this goal. At this stage you throw no punches. You are trying to use only footwork to manipulate your opponent's movement. Work this drill often.

Pressuring on the ropes

You have your opponent with his back to the ropes, and he is attempting to use his footwork to wheel out. Strive to keep him contained with only your side to side shuffling. Work for several rounds.

In the next stage of the drill you throw punches. Maintain a shuffle to keep your opponent against the ropes. When he attempts to wheel out, fire low hooks to keep him boxed in. Fire hooks only against the direction of his movement. For example, if he is shuffling to his left (your right) fire a low right hook to keep him trapped.

In the next version of the drill, fire high hooks to keep him trapped.

And finally, double-hook your opponent as he attempts to wheel out.

Optimally, during this drill you move laterally along the ring ropes keeping your opponent pinned with hooks and changing his direction at will.

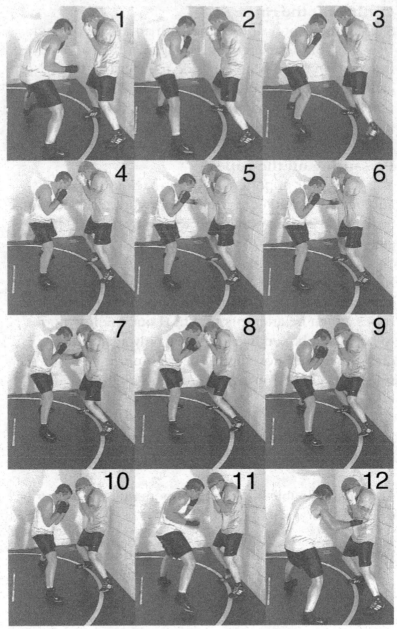

Pressuring on the ropes.

Cornering.

Cornering

This is the act of getting your man trapped with his back to the turnbuckle. You can accomplish this with your previous cutting off the ring and shuffling foot-work. Once you have your man cornered, it is time to tee off. Go to work with heavy combination work and use the shuffle to keep him boxed when he attempts to wheel out. If there was ever a time to push for the knockout or finish, this is it.

To drill this concept, use cutting off the ring drills and shuffling to pin a training partner and have him feed combination openings. Remember, you can really press the attack at this point.

20 Caught on the ropes

You do not ever want to be cornered or caught on the ropes. Your job is to control the center of the ring and to corner or catch your opponent on the ropes. But sometimes you may find yourself in that position or on the way there. The following tips and drills will provide your escape plan.

● When you are on the ropes, you are trapped. Get out ASAP. Do not fight off of the ropes. Do not rope-a-dope.

● Getting out is quite difficult, especially with a smart fighter in front of you who knows how to shuffle and corner well.

● Strive to hold the center of the ring and have a good sense of how close you are to the ropes at all times.

● When you feel the bottom ring rope touch your calf, it is time to move laterally and get out. (NHB fighters in cage situations should move laterally as soon as they feel their heel touch the cage wall.)

Sugar Ray Robinson drill.

● As you move laterally, jab and throw combinations, do not shell up. You must box your way back to the center.

The following drills address escapes while being driven toward the ropes and once you are on the ropes. Work each for several rounds.

Sugar Ray Robinson drill
As you are driven back, take a retreating step and then a swift side step to bring yourself out of danger.

Archie Moore drill
Shell up, place your head on his chest to cut off punching room and then move out to whichever side is open.

Jersey Joe Walcott drill
Shell, turn to your inside and step out.

Jim Jeffries drill
Shell, wheel/pivot to your outside and step out.

Archie Moore drill

Jersey Joe Walcott drill

Jim Jeffries drill

21 Infighting and shelling up

Some of the most vicious punching occurs during infighting so you must to be able to handle both the offensive and the defensive game at this range. Your infighting guard needs to be tight.

Here are a few considerations:
● Be ready to work inside your opponent's swings at the first opportunity. Use tight hooks, uppercuts, shovel hooks and short straight punches to beat his swings.

● Push his arms away from his body and follow up by hitting the body with tight hooks, uppercuts and shovel hooks.

● Use an active short rhythm once inside to foil his attempts to clinch.

● Remember to slip and move.

● When your opponent tries to clinch, rest your head against his chest and keep hitting the body with short, snappy punches.

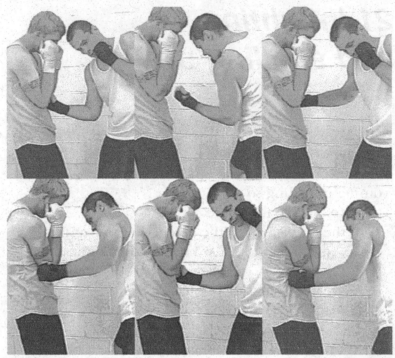

Use hooks, uppercuts, shovel and short straight punches to beat his swings.

● While placing your head on his chest, stay in control of your balance and weight. Don't lean into him, just touch his body with your head to prevent his clinch.

● Your best infighting weapons are hooks, uppercuts and shovel hooks.

● When in matched leads (both fighters have same lead), bump his lead shoulder with yours and then fire tight combinations such as rear uppercut, lead hook head, cross head, lead hook head (see next page).

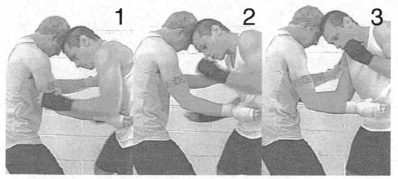

Avoiding his clinch by pushing his arms back ...

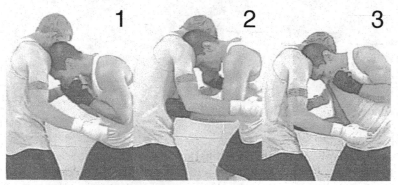

... and resting your head against his chest.

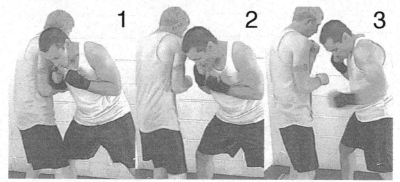

In matched leads bump his shoulder with yours and throw tight combinations.

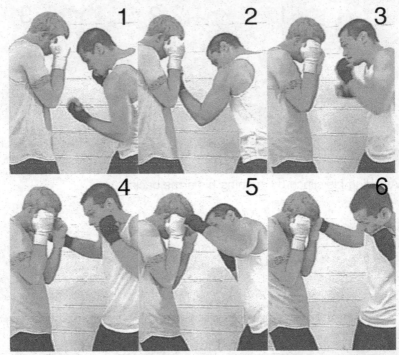

An excellent combination for infighting: rear uppercut, lead hook to the head, cross to the head and a lead hook to the head.

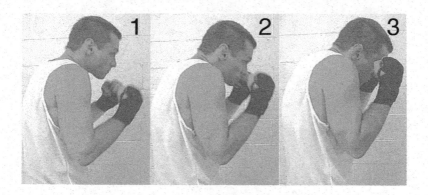

Shelling up
Shelling up is the defensive side of infighting.

● To shell up properly you need to tighten your guard even more than in offensive infighting. Completely cover the head and body. Leave no vulnerable area exposed.

● Just as you used the head in an offensive manner, it can be used in a defensive manner. Place your head on his chest to cut off punching room.

● It's best to get out of an infighting situation if you are unable to control it. Do this by wheeling out or using any of the tips in the Caught on the Ropes chapter.

Place your head on his chest to cut off punching room.

Shelling up.

22 Clinching

You see it in practically every fight and spectators hate to see it at all. The spectators are right. The purpose of a clinch is to get to a double-overhook position so that a fighter can muffle his opponent's attack. I do not advocate clinching since it is a poor defensive mechanism. You will exert three to four times as much energy clinching or attempting to clinch than you would if you simply blocked and moved. Most fighters clinch at a time when they can least afford this poor return on their effort.

So, is the clinch an absolute no-no? Not exactly. The clinch is a last resort defensive tactic. If you are going to clinch, make sure you do it right. But always keep this old gym maxim in mind — the clinch can keep you from losing, but it can never make you a winner.

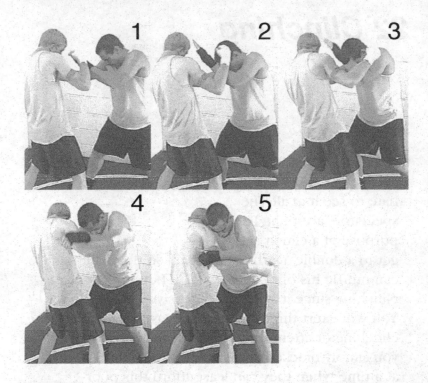

Standard clinch drill

The standard clinch entails over-hooking each of your opponent's arms with yours.

● You get into the clinch position with a breast stroke motion.

● It is ideal to overhook his arms just above the elbows with the crooks of your arms.

● Lay as much weight upon your opponent as you can. You can rest briefly, which tires him by making him carry your weight and better muffle his punches.

Spinning out

Getting out
There are two ways to safely leave the clinch.

Spin out drill
● You use the palm of one hand to grip your opponent just above the elbow.

● As you step away, shove the gripped arm across his chest at a downward 45 degree angle to upset any following attack he may launch.

Shove out drill

● Place your lead hand in the center of your opponent's chest.

● Once the hand is placed, shove him and step out of the clinch.

● The shove sets him on his heels and takes away prime punching position.

23 Ring generalship

Boxing is not only a physical game, it is, indeed, a mental one. And I'm not talking about the mental toughness necessary to be a serious competitor. I'm referring to the strategy of the ring, all the inside information you need for insight to what's going on (or should be going on) inside the squared circle like the pros and top trainers see it. I strongly recommend that you return to this section again and again to thoroughly digest all of the tips. Give as much time to commit strategy to memory as you do committing technique to muscle memory.

Tips
The following tips, in random order, range from thoughts on keeping your cool, to further drill ideas, to strategic advice on how to approach different types of fighters. Dig in and highlight what seems immediately useful. Return often as new sparring situations will bring other thoughts into bold relief.

● Before sparring it is wise to break a sweat. Warmed up muscles have faster reaction times. A few rounds of shadowboxing are usually sufficient to warm up a conditioned fighter.

● Always wrap the hands properly before sparring or working any equipment. Your hands are fragile and once injured, you will be out for a while. Always err on the side of safety.

● Coating the face with Vaseline reduces the chances of being cut. Most cuts occur when the dry leather of a boxing glove catches the dry skin of the face and tears it. The important areas to coat with Vaseline are the bridge of the nose, under and around the eyes, the cheeks, the lips, the chin and the ears. Many fighters forget to coat the ears. Trust me, ear rips are quite painful.

● Never compromise your defensive guard. It is common to see fighters square off against an opponent — planting the feet directly in front of him and facing him with the chest. Avoid this. Use the tried and true guards. Don't be a sloppy slugger. Be a boxer.

● Proper technique beats flashy technique and showboating every time.

● Strive to be an intelligent boxer and not a one-punch knockout artist. The overwhelming majority of knockouts come from diligent attention to the fundamentals of boxing, not from looking for the perfect time to tee off.

● Avoid telegraphing your intentions. Telegraphing is any telltale physical movement that indicates what your next punch or defensive action is going to be. Throw your punches crisply and cleanly without tipping your hand with head or shoulder movements or flying elbows. Fire from where your hand is.

● Don't be predictable. Mix up your offensive and defensive style so that your opponent can't read patterns.

● Punch at every opportunity. Do not reach, pat or paw at your opponent. This is a sign of indecision. Punch cleanly and often.

● Don't hesitate. If you start a punch, finish it. It may land or at least disrupt a counter. Half a punch is worthless.

● Don't flinch. This is easier said than done. Learn to keep your eyes open and on your opponent even under fire.

● Fights are won in the gym, not in the ring. Always be in top condition. It takes time and lots of training to build fighting stamina. The time spent is worth it. You can be the strongest, fastest, toughest boxer around but if the gas tank is empty you can be beaten by a chump.

● Groove each and every offensive and defensive technique into your nervous system. You do this through diligent repetitive training. Don't be anxious to move to the next drill until you have mastered what came before. Slow and sloppy technique is useless.

● Don't dance, prance or bounce around the ring. Utilize good footwork and don't waste your precious energy with showboat shuffles.

● Relax between rounds. This is a lot tougher than it seems because adrenaline from the fight can keep your system racing during that vital one minute break. Learn to regain as much composure and energy as you can.

● Anger leads to mistakes. A thinking fighter is an impassive fighter. There is no place for anger in sparring.

● Don't charge. Charging is usually the sign of a frustrated fighter who can think of no other way to get inside. If you charge, an experienced boxer will cut you down to size, pronto.

● Spar for the following reasons: You want to improve your skills. You want to have fun. You want to do your best to win. Never spar because you want to hurt someone. Boxing is a sport. A tough sport, yes, but a sport all the same. Spar to be a great sportsman.

● We've discussed that you must get used to the idea of getting hit. Well, you also need to get used to the idea of hitting another human being. Strangely enough, we all know that this is what this sport is about, yet some great competitors, initially, are hesitant to do so. It's a part of the game. Hit or be hit.

● Any time you enter a new or different ring, get familiar with it. Move on it, get a feel for the surface, the ropes and its size. Each ring is slightly different. Get used to it before you fight. Once you hear the bell, your only concern should be your opponent.

● Reach can be deceptive. Look at your opponent's arms, not his reach measurements. Reach is measured fingertip to fingertip with arms outstretched. The measurement therefore includes extended fingers and the width of the torso. This inclusion makes this number meaningless sometimes.

● When struck in the head, strive to respond with the entire body. Using the whole body acts as a shock absorber. Moving only the head increases the risk of neck injury.

● Chuck Bodak, a former coach of Muhammad Ali, said, "I'm a firm believer that you should watch the hands of your opponent. Trying to decipher his intentions by watching his shoulders and feet causes mass confusion. He doesn't hit you with his shoulders and feet. He hits you with his hands."

● Use the jab as an information probe. Start the fight with the jab to see what he does. If he responds the same way two or three times in a row, then more than likely, that response is a habit. Capitalize on it.

● Be confident. If you don't feel confident, fake it. If you've trained hard in the gym, you won't be faking for long.

● Keep moving. A stationary target is an easy target.

● Maintain your guard at all times.

● Never give up the science. Stay with your gym-trained game plan.

● Whenever your opponent is in range, punch. Don't hesitate, punch. If you are in range to punch, he is in range to punch. Be there first.

● Never fight your opponent's game. In other words, don't slug with a slugger, don't counterpunch with a counterpuncher. Train all styles diligently. You'll have one you excel in, but be confident and competent in all of them.

● You will miss more than you will hit. Recover your balance, stay covered and hit again.

● When you see your opponent getting set to hit, move. Always move. Stick and move means punch and move. Never stay still. Use footwork and rhythm.

● If you have reach on your opponent, use this to your advantage and jab incessantly.

● Observe fight films of the past masters and watch the masters of today for inspiration and learning.

Boxing the tall opponent may include ducking his jab and throwing crosses to the body.

Boxing the tall opponent

● Attempt to make him come to you. Most tall boxers are used to playing on the outside and making their opponent's come to them. See if you can reverse this situation and make him come to you.

● If he will not come to you, move in whenever possible and work the body. Remain there or, at least, get in often if this is successful. Working from the inside eliminates his height advantage.

● Once inside, use all the tips and drills from the infighting section to work the body and head.

● You will have to work off his jab. Master defending the jab with catching, blocking and cuffing. Once you feel his jab make contact, get inside immediately.

● Drill slipping and ducking the tall fighter's jabs and crosses and countering with crosses to the body. Drill this in the gym before you face the tall fighter.

● Use explosive in and out movements, with short, powerful punches thrown to the body and head. Emphasize hooks, uppercuts and shovel hooks.

● Observe masters of this in-out style such as Roberto Duran, Rocky Marciano, Henry Armstrong, Joe Frazier, Jack Dempsey, Julio Cesar Chavez and Mike Tyson.

Stepping and pivoting around the straight charger and delivering a lead uppercut.

Boxing the charger and infighter
● Keep moving.

● Don't fight his fight.

● Side step, pivot, waltz and stick him with the jab whenever and wherever possible. Follow the jab with a cross.

● If he gets inside, shell up and immediately move outside.

● Avoid the clinch. In the time that you strive to grab him, you can get your body battered and have your energy sapped.

● Work the jab incessantly. Double and triple up on them to break his rhythm.

● Stick and move.

● Keep circling. Most infighters prefer to move straight ahead. Do not provide him with that opportunity.

● Make him back up with your incessant jabs. Few infighters and chargers move or punch well while stepping back.

● Along with jabs, fire quick, snappy crosses, hooks and uppercuts. If (that's a big if) you are very quick, use the occasional leading rear straight.

● Observe masters of this style such as Sugar Ray Robinson, Muhammad Ali, Gene Tunney, Willie Pep and Sugar Ray Leonard.

● I also recommend you study great matchups between these two types of fighters. Study Ali and Frazier, Robinson and LaMotta, Dempsey and Tunney, Leonard and Duran, and Douglas and Tyson.

With hands high and in proper guard position, you can cuff or catch the jab and counter.

Boxing the jab artist

● Keep the rear hand in proper guard position to catch and cuff his jabs. Be prepared to slip and duck his jab to infight or to counter with a quick punch to the head or body.

● Work the body to sap his energy. Cut the ring off and attempt to corner or put him on the ropes in order to take his jab range away.

Straight punches beat wide punches every time.

Boxing the slugger

● Don't slug with the slugger. It's a crap shoot at best and most usually in his favor. Play your game, not his.

● Keep moving. Do not let the slugger get set to fire his bombs. Move in quickly for sudden attacks and get out just as quickly. Don't stay inside playing his range.

Boxing the southpaw or unmatched leads

● Don't lead. Make the southpaw come to you.

● Circle away from his rear hand. Always keep your rear hand high and ready to catch the rear bomb.

● Gain superior footwork position by placing your lead foot to the outside of your opponent's lead foot.

● A primary weapon with the southpaw is the lead hook. When he throws his jab, slip outside and fire this punch.

● You should break one of the primary rules of boxing when fighting a southpaw by leading with the rear hand. Use feints and rear hand leads to set up combinations utilizing both hands.

● Other than the lead hook (used like the jab against an orthodox fighter) your most important weapons will be rear hooks, crosses, rear uppercuts, rear shovel hooks and lead uppercuts.

● When two southpaws face, the standard rules apply and the jab again becomes the primary weapon.

Work these drills to prepare for the unmatched lead
(see next two pages):

● Step outside, rear hook body, lead hook head
● Cross head, lead hook head
● Cross head, lead hook body

Unmatched lead combo one — Stepping outside, fire a rear hook to the body and a lead hook to the head.

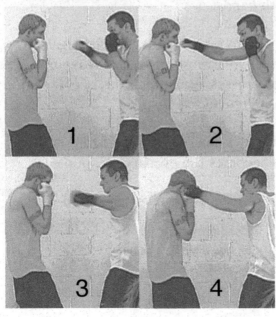

Unmatched lead combo two — Cross to the head and a lead hook to the head.

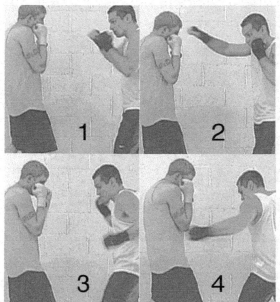

Unmatched lead combo three — Cross to the head followed by a lead hook to the body.

Patience may be valuable in the face of a flurry.

Boxing the speed demon

● Don't let an opponent's seemingly overwhelming speed daunt you. The speed demon is as overrated as the fighter who hunts only for the knockout opportunity.

● Timing beats speed. Directed attack beats the furious flurry. Timing and directed attack are learned by long hours in the gym and will serve you well against this or any other opponent.

Resources

For questions about this material or for more training information and frequent updates to this book, please go to my Web site www.extreme-selfprotection.com.

Books

As mentioned in the introduction, there are few contemporary boxing texts (real boxing, not fitness boxing) on the market. In the past, there were many. Today, we are limited to the following:

Boxer's Start-Up: A Beginner's Guide to Boxing by Doug Werner

Fighting Fit: Boxing Workouts, Techniques and Sparring by Doug Werner and Alan Lachica

No Holds Barred Fighting: Savage Strikes by Mark Hatmaker

This is directed at the NHB fighter, but the introductory chapters contain much information pertinent to boxing.

Equipment

Everlast 718-993-0100

Ringside
1-877-4-BOXING
www.ringside.com

Video instruction

Paladin Press
www.paladin-press.com
See *Extreme Boxing* and *Extreme Boxing Chain Drills* by Mark Hatmaker

Threat Response Solutions
www.trsdirect.com
See *Illegal Boxing* by Mark Hatmaker

Index

More titles by Mark Hatmaker
www.extremeselfprotection.com

Also available at all major bookstores

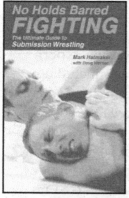

**No Holds Barred Fighting
The Ultimate Guide
to Submission Wrestling**
Mark Hatmaker
1-884654-17-7 / $12.95
The combat art of The Ultimate Fighting
Championships. 695 photos.

**More No Holds Barred Fighting:
Killer Submissions**
Mark Hatmaker
1-884654-18-5 / $12.95
More takedowns, rides and submissions
from the authors of *No Holds Barred
Fighting*. 650 photos.

**No Holds Barred Fighting:
Savage Strikes**
The Complete Guide to Real World
Striking for NHB Competition
and Street Defense
Mark Hatmaker
1-884654-20-7 / $12.95
Punches, kicks, forearm shots, head
butts and more. 850 photos.

Mark Hatmaker is the author of *No Holds Barred Fighting*, *More No Holds Barred Fighting: Killer Submissions* and *No Holds Barred Fighting: Savage Strikes*. He also has produced over 20 instructional videos. His resume includes extensive experience in the combat arts including boxing, wrestling, Jiujitsu and Muay Thai. He is a highly regarded coach of professional and amateur fighters, law enforcement officials and security personnel. Hatmaker is founder of Extreme Self Protection (ESP), a research body that compiles, analyzes and teaches the most effective western combat methods known. ESP holds numerous seminars throughout the country each year, including the prestigious Karate College/Martial Arts Universities in Radford, Virginia. He lives in Knoxville, Tennessee.

More books and videos by Mark Hatmaker
www.extremeselfprotection.com

Books are also available at all major bookstores